Sutton

IN OLD PHOTOGRAPHS

Sutton

IN OLD PHOTOGRAPHS

PATRICIA BERRY

Alan Sutton Publishing Limited
Phoenix Mill · Far Thrupp · Stroud
Gloucestershire

First Published 1994

Copyright © Patricia Berry, 1994

British Library Cataloguing in Publication Data.
A catalogue record for this book is available from
the British Library.

ISBN 0-7509-0646-4

Typeset in 9/10 Sabon.
Typesetting and origination by
Alan Sutton Publishing Limited.
Printed in Great Britain by
Ebenezer Baylis, Worcester.

Contents

Church Road (now redeveloped and known as St Nicholas Way), *c.* 1900.

Introduction

The London borough of Sutton stretches north to Morden and Mitcham, south to Banstead Downs, Belmont, Woodmansterne and Purley, and from Worcester Park in the west to Beddington in the east. It is a far cry from the tiny settlement of Sudtone (meaning south farm or village) which William I's clerk found when he arrived there twenty years after the Norman Conquest. His task was to record for the king's census (known as the Domesday Book) population, land, livestock and value; he found that a small agricultural community of some two hundred souls existed in a region held by the Abbot of Chertsey.

The village progressed quietly under the patronage of the abbey, with few alterations, till Tudor times. In 1538 Henry VIII was immersed in his plan to break up the monasteries which held so much power and land; he was also involved in the building of Nonsuch, his magnificent palace at Cuddington. He then acquired the manor of Sutton, less than 2 miles away, and presented it to Sir Nicholas Carew. Though that surname still survives in the part-medieval Carew Manor in Beddington Park, the family's tenure of Sutton was very brief. Over the next three hundred years ownership was periodically purchased or bequeathed, until it was acquired in 1845 by Mr Thomas Alcock. By this time the little town was gradually extending from its original site around the parish church, though keeping to the strip of Thanet sand where water was readily obtainable. To the north and south, even where crossed by the turnpike road, there was little habitation, for beneath the fields and downs was chalk or clay, and water could not come to the surface.

That turnpike, laid in 1755, would have accounted for some of the livelier days of Sutton's existence, when coaches came through en route from London to the south coast. The Prince Regent (later George IV) passed that way; it was he who ordered the cutting through steep Angel Hill, and he kept his own Rockingham china tea service at the Cock Hotel, ready for his refreshment while his coach horses were swapped. Sutton also lay on the road to Epsom Downs and, with the rise to popularity of the Derby and other race meetings, the Cock became the centre of riotous festivities. The inn has the distinction of being the only named feature in mid-Victorian short-story writer Angus Reach's colourful description of the Derby day 'pilgrimage', in what is generally recognized as the earliest thriller about that race.

Thomas Alcock's projects to construct new roads and sell land in the area to development companies coincided with the London, Brighton and South Coast Railway's decision to extend their London Bridge–West Croydon line to Epsom. These events encouraged families and businesses to settle, and the 1861 census revealed that the town's population had increased five-fold in fifty years.

The expansion began to the east of the turnpike, where the New Town grew up around Jenny Lind Road and Benhill (later St Barnabas) Road, turnings off Carshalton Road which itself had been no more than a track through fields till made up into a half-width turnpike. Here stood The Elms, a flint-built villa that would soon become the office of the water company, whose pumping station and mains system enabled development to the south, on each side of Brighton Road, from 1864.

As the nineteenth century drew to a close, tree-lined avenues of detached houses developed on all sides of the old town centre. Owners were usually city businessmen, and one or two writers and artists; their wives and daughters led a genteel life of church-going, concerts, conversaziones, tennis, telescope parties and good works among the poor, while their sons concentrated on being educated. The wants of all of them were ministered to by an army of cooks and maid-servants. It is from those Lizzies and Dorries, Minnies and Nellies that details of so many authentic scenes and so much about everyday attitudes and comments have come, for they kept up a jolly grapevine of news among themselves by postcard (the Edwardian equivalent of telephone gossip). How one can sympathize with the young woman, transported from the street cries of London to the quiet of Sutton, who wrote: 'Pity me polishing oil cloth today, but it's a treat to hear the birds in the morning instead of sweep sweep coals coals rags bottles any old lumber.'

By the First World War, Sutton High Street, while keeping its place as the main artery of the town, had undergone great changes. Private homes such as Sutton Court, Sutton Manor, Garden House and Slate House had been demolished or converted to make room for shops, replacing the old cottage-style premises of Mr Stevens the bootmaker, Mr Farrance the bird stuffer and Mr Brown the butcher. This was the High Street which my mother knew, when she ran errands from Belmont before school in the mornings. A surprising number of these rebuilt shops have survived, as a glance at upstairs windows and façades will prove, though shopfronts may have been modernized several times.

It was regarded as a great step forward in Sutton's history when, with Cheam, it received borough status in 1934, with an estimated population of almost 77,000. I was then a small girl and have only snapshot memories of the charter celebrations, but I clearly recall Sutton as a shopping and entertainment centre at that time. Shinner's was the big department store with the latest fashions, the smartest window-dressing, the oddest 'stunts' to promote their new lines. We were spoiled for choice with three cinemas, the Plaza (later Granada), the County (later Gaumont) and Cheam Road Picture Theatre.

In the course of a century, farmland, lavender fields, downland, private estates and parkland have disappeared beneath bricks and mortar, but a town's history is also made by its people and their development through religion, education, home life and recreation. Younger residents and newcomers to what became a London borough in 1965 may know only present-day Sutton with its ringroad, civic centre and shopping malls, and want nothing else; each generation will have its own memories and tastes. I hope there is something for everyone in this chronicle of Sutton's past one hundred years.

This book represents far more than one woman's work; it is the result of support and encouragement from a number of people, acknowledged either in the text or on p. 160. If anyone has been missed, or any photographic source not cleared, apologies are tendered for the oversight.

Patricia Berry
Seaford, East Sussex

SECTION ONE

The High Street

Jubilee Arch near the railway station, 1887. This faded snapshot, slotted into the back of a postcard, is marked 'Queen Victoria's Golden Jubilee, Sutton Station and High Street looking north'. On the extreme left is the Station Hotel, still a public house today though with another name. On the right behind the cart is Bowling's the ironmongers, festooned with bunting. They moved to Grove Road thirty-nine years later, and the Midland Bank moved in.

Looking towards Grove Road, Christmas 1907. On the left, near the boy with the bicycle, is Wootten Brothers' select draper's shop, opened in about 1882. My mother remembers, as a girl, frequently seeing Mr Robert Wootten standing in the shop doorway greeting customers, always with a bunch of violets on his coat lapel. It is said that instead of giving money for these to the flower seller on the corner of Grove Road he would provide her with a new overcoat each winter. Mr Wootten was president of Sutton United football club for several years before the First World War. Riddington's sign on the extreme right marks the shop and restaurant which occupied these premises for very many years. The same firm had a bakery in one of the old shops opposite the Cock Hotel.

Opposite: The London and Provincial Bank, 1905. Twenty-five years earlier both the High Street and Cheam Road toll-gates would have been visible in a photograph taken from this angle. The bank has changed very little; at ground-floor level it now extends into the shop occupied by the Royal Dairy. The large square lantern protruding into the picture on the left belongs to the Cock Hotel; both the Greyhound and the Grapes lower down the High Street followed this tradition of illuminating their frontages and the road outside.

Opposite the Cock Hotel, 1888. The building with the bow window upstairs was known first as the Railway Tavern, and later as the Green Man. Among the characters outside is one readily identifiable as a coachman by his high hat and leggings. The house and shop with steps up were later occupied by another bakery, Riddington's, where my grandmother served while my grandfather tended the delivery horses, kept in stables at the back. The stables still existed in the 1950s, part of a bombed site used for Civil Defence practice.

Looking south to the Cock Hotel, *c.* 1890. The old hotel had stood since the days of stagecoaches, when it was a posting station for the change of horses on the 40-mile London–Brighton route. The wooden arch across the road carried the sign of a cockerel, perhaps indicating that cock-fights used to be held at the inn. A toll-gate barred the Brighton Road – close to the spot where the six men (with bicycle) are standing – until the mid-nineteenth century, when it moved further south as housing developed in that direction. The building on the far left was the original taproom, and the new Cock Hotel was built on that site in 1897.

The Cock Hotel, 1906. The new hotel boasted a magnificent first-floor dining-room, reached by a staircase from its own street door. The forecourt was separated from the High Street by a narrow strip of pavement, for years the site of a newspaper stand. Behind the postman and policeman is the double lamp standard supporting the old inn sign, complete with metal cockerel perched on top. The inn has survived, although the hotel was demolished in 1961. On the far corner of Carshalton Road is William Pile's three-storey bookshop and stationer's; next door down the hill, Fisher's the men's outfitter has a comprehensive stock list painted on the wall.

Mrs Evelyn Burns of Victoria Road walking near the municipal offices, in the High Street, 1930. Zeeta's sign advertising teas and luncheons may remind older readers of that very pleasant cake shop and restaurant.

Looking north, 1910. On early street maps, this part of the High Street is designated 'the Cock Hill'. In stagecoach days, this was the last steep pull to the hotel where the horses were changed, and men and beasts would have welcomed the sight. The two inked crosses in the centre of this postcard are, according to the sender, 'Charlie's shop'; quite soon the whole parade would belong to Mr Ernest Shinner.

The view north from Cheam Road, c. 1910. Graham's wine and spirit shop on the north corner of the road to Cheam had already been on this site for some thirty years when this postcard was sent, but the building has been occupied by Lloyd's Bank for a very long time. The upper storeys of most buildings in this part of the High Street retain the window and roof formations as originally designed, though their shop fronts may have been updated several times.

W.R. Church's bookshop and stationer's, 1880. Only twelve years earlier, this site had been part of the spacious grounds of Hill House, the home of Mr R. Still; some of the shops then built stand in 1994. Part of the new London and Provincial Bank (manager Mr T. Bartlett) shows on the extreme left. The transfer of the branch to larger, purpose-built premises was interpreted as proof of the town's growing importance; within twenty-five years another move was necessary. On the right is Hill Road, with the flint-faced Baptist chapel erected in 1873 at a cost of £2,250 including furnishings – and fences. (*See also* p. 43.)

Local government, *c.* 1930. Sutton Urban District Council, formed in 1894, moved into the new municipal offices (left) on the corner of Throwley Road about seven years later. This imposing building continued to serve as the hub of local government through borough status to London Borough until its demolition in 1970. The coat of arms (below) belongs to the Talbot family, some eighteenth-century members of which are entombed in St Nicholas' churchyard. They include the first Earl Talbot created in 1761; the heraldic hounds are a play on words of his surname.

The Arcade leading to Throwley Road, 1920s. Today a number of the shops are empty, but the bright light through the glass roof and the unique echoing of voices and footfalls below have not changed. Mr Shinner built the arcade as part of his department store; after shopping hours, the commissionaire drew out and locked folding metal gates at each end. A favourite window in the 1930s was the milliner's: each special hat bore a small sign saying 'as worn by Joan Crawford' (or Janet Gaynor, Ginger Rogers or some other Hollywood film star). Until the Second World War most women wore hats for all outdoor occasions.

Shinners Restaurant advertisement, 1948. A lift worked by an attendant carried patrons to the top-floor restaurant. As advertised, the room was large enough for dinner-dances and receptions; some of Sutton's first post-Second World War fashion shows were held there.

Looking south from below St Nicholas Road, 1904. In the centre is Amos Reynolds' furnishing and undertaker's corner premises (formerly Easton and Truncheon cabinet-maker's), acquired seventy-five years ago as part of Allder's store, and since re-developed. On the extreme left is the sign of the Paragon at no. 112 (see below). Top right, the Electric Theatre sign shows the way (now an access way near Boot's the chemist) to a small movie house, eclipsed in 1920 by the High Street Picture Palace, built almost opposite.

Looking north from St Nicholas Road, 1900. The railings on the extreme right stood in front of the police station, immediately beyond the tiny Paragon newsagent's and sweet shop that jutted out towards the kerb. People passing by often caught their arms on the newspaper rack that hung outside. The patch of sunlight across the pavement marks the entrance to the steam mills, and the corresponding gap across the High Street by the lamppost led into Mr Leeding's 'Sutton Carriage Works, established 1829', which continued in business until 1967.

The old police station, 1909. Police headquarters had already occupied this site for thirty years, but moved soon after to 6 Carshalton Road where, as a sub-divisional Metropolitan Police station, it has one inspector, nine sergeants and fifty-six constables. Behind the building stood a windmill, which later became Napper's steam flour-mills. It was well signposted by the small shop on the corner, with festoons of oats, wheat and barley stalks decorating the windows.

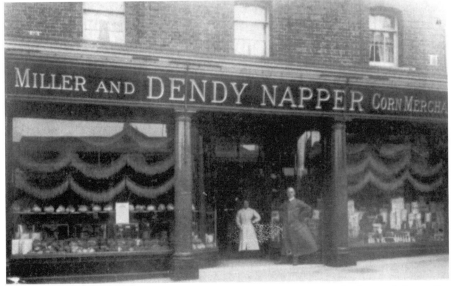

Dendy Napper's bakery. Comparison of the upper windows with those of the police station (above) shows that only the ground floor required major alteration to make this double-fronted shop. The festoons, changed annually, continued to adorn the windows for many years. Inside there was a pleasantly dusty, yeasty atmosphere, but it was the display of tropical fish in their tanks that always claimed my attention, while Mother shopped for a 'split tin' or 'sliced sandwich' loaf (the slicing ordered in advance).

Looking north from Greyhound Corner, mid-1920s. This postcard view contains a mixture of architectural fashions, at a time when modern shops were replacing the old converted cottages. Far left, on the corner of West Street, are the premises occupied by Mr Fraser's ironmonger's; in the 1930s they were replaced by John Perring's five-storey furniture emporium. The smaller shop next door had earlier been Grace Cottages; one of the tall buildings with 'stepped' gables survives to this day. Another feature of this scene is the lime tree on the extreme right which succumbed only in 1994.

The Grapes Hotel on the corner of Benhill Street. The inn, opened in around 1896, advertises 'Brandy importer, wine and spirit merchant – Whitbread and Co's London porter'. Deliveries were made through the opening on the left (now blocked up), which was decorated with intricate ironwork tracery. In 1906 a tram route with overhead wires was laid from Croydon to Sutton, terminating outside the inn (*see also* the Transport section, pp. 60–2). The leafy tree on the left stood on the opposite corner, while just visible on the right is another of the large lanterns which helped to illuminate the road as well as drawing attention to the inn itself. The inn is now called The Corner House.

Looking south from Haddon Road, *c.* 1907. The tree in the centre stands on the corner of Benhill Street opposite the Grapes Hotel (above). The two policemen on the far right are about to cross Greenford Road. Large exterior lamps are in evidence once again and a number of shops advertise their wares by hanging samples outside. Many upper-storey windows have changed little in almost ninety years, although the shop fronts have been modernized.

Looking north from Marshalls Road, Christmas 1910. The tradition of seasonal street decorations has here been used to let off some political steam, the point at issue now long forgotten. The tall chimney-stacks of the Red Lion Inn are far left; although there is a lamp standard nearby, the inn retains its own large lantern outside. The lower inn sign (a cyclist alongside) belongs to the Crown, on the south corner of Crown Road.

Christmas decorations, looking south from Crown Road, 1907. A wide range of services is offered by shops near the junction with Marshalls Road, to the left. As well as stationery, hardware, chandlery, ironmongery and furniture on the left, on the far right are places where one could not only receive a shave or hair-cut, but even have umbrellas nursed back to health. The frontage of the new Red Lion Inn is just visible with a ladder and men fixing the decorations; the old tavern, immediately to the south, had been demolished that year.

Opposite Crown Road. On the right are the business premises of registered plumber George S. Webb, who also advertised himself as 'painter, glazier, gas-fitter, hot-water engineer, electric and crank-bell fitter'. The low wall to the right of the horses formed the boundary of Mr Webb's yard, where pipes and other building materials were stored. The ground floor of the weather-boarded house was later converted, the northern part into a tobacconist's, the rest becoming a shop offering dressmaker's services such as pleating and picot-edging, and 'hem-stitching while you wait'. The building stood until around 1932, when new shops were erected.

SECTION TWO

The Green and Angel Hill

Looking north-east to All Saints' church, 1905. This view of well-mown grass with intersecting roads and surrounding greenery remains basically unchanged, although some of the trees have been removed or replaced, some of the houses rebuilt, and only one of the smart white posts survives.

The Pond. A weeping willow 'coronation tree' was planted to commemorate Queen Victoria's crowning in 1838. Other trees serving as royal remembrances were an elm for the Queen's jubilee sixty years later and an oak for the coronation of her son Edward VII in 1901. The Victoria pond was earmarked as an emergency water source during the Second World War, but was drained in the mid-1950s and the site turned into a small park. The tree on the right (with notice attached) has survived to the present time, as have the Cricketers Inn, with its older weather-boarded part at the rear, and the High Street shops on the far right. Other buildings were damaged or destroyed when bombs fell in the area of Vale Road/Crown Road/Sutton Creameries dairy.

Looking south-west from High Street, 1905. This is the counterpart view to the photograph on p. 25, and includes 5 The Green, the former farmhouse now divided into flats. The writer of his postcard described the trees as 'lovely old elms close to the Angel Bridge'.

Angel Bridge looking south, 1910. The Sutton Gas Company was established in 1857 and was the main supplier of domestic fuel for lighting, heating and cooking until electricity became readily available from around 1902. A gasometer still stands on the Crown Road site.

The drinking fountain, 1918. The fountain was erected on the Green to commemorate the coronation of Edward VII (as was the oak tree by the pond). All that now remains is a slight indentation in the grass, and even many older inhabitants have forgotten it ever stood there. The corner house on the right is 1 Bushey Road.

Skinner's farm, 1906. Mr W. Skinner, dairyman, had already occupied Hall Mead Farm for more than twenty years when this postcard was produced.

The view from Stayton Road, 1930s. Fairs and circuses sometimes set up on the Green in the years before the Second World War, when the grass was bounded on all sides by chain slung between neat white posts. A political rally was once held there by Oswald Mosley. A public air-raid shelter was excavated in the north-east corner in the early days of the war; such shelters had large signs outside – a white letter S on a black background – and were in the charge of wardens. People caught in the street when the sirens sounded, warning of the approach of enemy aircraft, were advised to scurry below ground for safety.

Angel Hill and the old bridge. These two views, looking north (above) and south (below), illustrate how a cutting was made through the hill, to build an easier road for horse-drawn traffic. The tradition is that this was done at the behest of the Prince Regent, who in 1820 became King George IV; he often travelled to Brighton on this road. The old bridge was built before the days of open-topped double-decker buses, hence a warning had to be painted on it in the early 1930s: 'Low bridge – bus passengers remain seated'.

Benhill Road, 1906. This name was originally given to the entire road from the junction of Angel Hill, running due east and curving south to Lower Road. It skirted the wooded Benhill on the west, with lavender fields and open land dotted with brickfields on the other side. Houses had names such as The Limes, Hazeldean and Oak Villa.

Cressingham Grove, 1906. An old map of around 1870 shows that the Benhill was crowned with trees and only Benhillwood Road, the eastern part of Oakhill Road and Cressingham Grove, existed at that time. The names, and the many trees to be seen in both these views, indicate the rural atmosphere of those days.

The Angel Inn, 1915 and 1940. This hostelry existed in the days when the Prince Regent drove along the Brighton road, and no doubt he took advantage of the fact, when his entourage paused to give their horses a 'breather' before tackling the hill. The broad path in front of the inn is part of the old, steep road; the cutting is edged with bushes and railings.

Rosehill recreation ground, 1950s. In sharp contrast to the bowls tournaments played near the park gate, Sutton's own baseball team had their diamond on the field near the railway line. As well as local men, players included expatriate Canadians and Americans. Among their opponents were the Epsom Lions, the Leatherhead Maple Leafs, the Wellingborough Indians, Kodak, the US Navy (Grosvenor Square) and the US Air Force (Ruislip). The borough's junior tennis centre and all-weather pitch now occupy that area.

Personnel of Post E3, Aultone Way, 1946. High-explosive, incendiary and flying bombs fell in the Sutton area in the Second World War, killing and injuring hundreds of people and rendering many more homeless. The Air-Raid Precautions organization (later renamed Civil Defence), set up in 1938 when war seemed imminent, worked in rescue, evacuation, advice, communications and general welfare of the community.

Construction of St Helier Hospital, 1937–8. The hospital's main entrance was in Wrythe Lane, in the south-east part of Rosehill Park. It started with over 700 beds; Sutton and Cheam General Hospital in Banstead Road, Belmont, had opened in 1931 with a mere sixty-eight. It is possible that the Rose Hill took its name from an early attempt to grow quantities of roses there for use in the manufacture of perfume, but without the success of the local lavender fields. The area also appears as Fern Hill on some old maps.

Christmas Fair at the Baptist Hall, 1963. On this occasion funds raised by the St Helier Hospital League of Friends went towards the provision of a three-channel radio service for patients. League President Harry (now Sir Harry) Secombe opened proceedings and spoke about present social conditions in contrast to those of Charles Dickens's time, arising from his West End appearances as Mr Pickwick. He is pouring coffee for the Mayor of Sutton and Cheam, Alderman D.P. Thomas. (Published by kind courtesy of the Croydon Advertiser Group Ltd.)

Garendon Road, 1930s. The St Helier estate was named after a lady member of London County Council, which body proposed the creation of over 9,000 homes in an area of more than 800 acres, to rehouse families from inner London. Commemorating the original ownership of the land by the Church, the roads had the names of English abbeys. Studying a local street map reveals that the names are also roughly alphabetical, from north to south. A pleasant feature of the 'garden suburb' planning of the estate was the inclusion of small railed-off grass areas to open up the street corners.

SECTION THREE

Churches and Chapels

The parish church of St Nicholas, pre-1862. It is a thousand years since a church first stood in this part of the old village of Sudtone. The land was held by the monks of Chertsey whose abbot, John de Rutherwyk, ordered major alterations in the thirteenth century. In Tudor times bells, vestments and furnishings were sold to raise funds for urgent repairs, and two centuries later the wooden tower was rebuilt in brick at a cost of £600. At that time the church was 70 ft long and 38 ft wide.

The Gibson Mausoleum, 1970. This Portland stone tomb stands in the south-west corner of St Nicholas' churchyard. On 12 August each year an inspection ceremony takes place, in accordance with the 1786 will of Mrs Mary Gibson: '. . . £4 to be divided among the churchwardens on that day, on condition of their attending to the monument and family vault of the Gibsons'. Legend has it that an aged toad lives in the tomb, and is sometimes glimpsed during the annual ceremony.

Path through the parish churchyard, *c.* 1900. Although time and the 1987 hurricane have damaged some trees and tombstones, it is still possible to identify the Balchin, Williams, Clowser, Hobbs and Hunter family graves, among others. The vestry was added to this side of the church in 1893, at a cost of £1,400; at the same time the heating was improved and new altar rails and a north porch were provided. The Revd Herbert William Turner MA was then rector.

Interior of St Nicholas' church, 1906. A number of monuments and relics from the old church, which was rebuilt in 1864, were preserved and continue to be displayed, together with charity boards and later memorials. For many years the opening words of Psalm 122 – 'I was glad when they said unto me, Let us go into the house of the Lord' – were painted round the curve of the chancel arch. Also surviving from the thirteenth-century church is a piscina or small stone basin, now removed to the wall by the lady chapel steps. This view was published by E. Bathurst, bookseller and stationer, of 5 Grand Parade, High Street.

St Nicholas' church from the west, 1906. The Revd Henry Hatch was rector when building of the present church began, at a cost of £7,200. Sutton was expanding rapidly, the population of some 3,200 having almost tripled since the arrival of the railway in 1847.

St Nicholas' church from the south-east, 1906. Many of the tombstones on these two postcards can still be identified. This view, published by C.A. Welch of 163 Sutton High Street, conveys a message from 'Nellie': 'This is the church we attend where Lizzie is to be married next Monday.'

All Saints', Benhilton, 1904. Within twenty years of the coming of the railway to the town, the population had grown enough to warrant a second parish church. In 1863 Sutton was divided into the parishes of St Nicholas', Sutton, and All Saints', Benhilton; the latter church was built two years later on Angel Hill with 874 seats, half of them free.

Interior of All Saints', Benhilton. Enemy bombing in the Second World War destroyed the original east window and caused major damage. Restoration was not completed for twenty-five years, the stained glass eventually being replaced in 1964. The reredos was removed at about the same time.

All Saints' church and vicarage, 1908. The vicarage was built in an acre of glebe to the east of the church, for the first incumbent, the Revd John Booker MA. The bombing which damaged the church in 1944 had a worse effect on the vicarage, and completely destroyed the parish hall and adjoining school.

St Andrew's, The Wrythe. This small church, built as a chapel of ease in 1887, could accommodate a congregation of 250.

The Baptist church, High Street, 1909. The chapel on the extreme left was erected in Hill Road in 1873, and the tower and church the following year. The impressive flint building dominated this part of the High Street for over fifty years until it was overtaken by Mr Ernest Shinner's southward expansion of his department store. The Baptist congregation then moved into a new church in Cheam Road, almost opposite the Trinity Methodist church.

St Barnabas' church, New Town, from the north, 1916. At the far right is the school, opened at Advent 1881, more than two years before the church itself. The congregation was gathered from residents of the 'New Town' created on land to the east of old Sutton, around Jenny Lind Road (later called Lind Road). In that street a room was found where the first services and meetings were held. A building committee, undaunted by problems over patronage, fund-raising, architects' approval and appointment of a vicar, saw the new church through to consecration on Saturday 29 March 1884. In 1982 the garden in the foreground became the site of the new vicarage. The patronal festival is 11 June.

Sutton St Barnabas' football club, 1895. The church first formed a cricket team, soon followed by these footballers. Cricket colours chosen were claret and gold, but the suppliers' quote of 17s 6d per cap was rejected in favour of cheaper ones at 3s 6d each in chocolate and amber. St Barnabas' combined with Sutton Guild Rovers in 1898 to form Sutton United, whose colours are chocolate and amber to this day. Standing, left to right: W. Stevens, E.J. Quick, W. Rowley, Revd C.J. Boden MA (vicar), C. Leeding, W.G. Scott, E.C. Surridge. On bench, left to right: J. Blythe, W. Hassell, A. Turner, F. Seabrook, L. Pettitt. Seated on ground, left to right: E.F. Boorer, J. Winter. Turner is holding the Herald Cup, won that season.

Interior of St Barnabas' church, 1910. The clergy inset are Canon W. Bartlett (second vicar, 1896–1919) on the left, Mr Tonge (right, above) and Mr Anthony (below). The richly coloured east window remains (a product of the William Morris studio) but many other changes have taken place. The pulpit, still with its carving 'Thy will be done', is now by the south column of the chancel arch. The brass lectern was sent to a church in Nigeria, and replaced by a carved wooden one. The chancel walls were plastered over in 1934 and those of the nave after the Second World War. That conflict inspired a stained-glass window designed to honour local Civil Defence workers, and memorial panels in remembrance of the war dead. Very many other items have been given in memory of past members of the congregation, and Canon Bartlett himself was commemorated in 1952 by the addition of an oak cover to the font.

The first Salvation Army band, 1887. Captain Jackson and her sister arrived in Sutton to start a corps in 1886, eight years after the Revd W. Booth's Christian Mission became known as the Salvation Army. Having been refused the use of the public hall, Captain Jackson held her first meetings in a High Street shop. This drawing from the *War Cry* journal shows Sutton's one drummer and four tin-whistle players who marched at Alexandra Palace among better appointed bands, in front of the Army's founder. Though their early appearances were greeted with derision and catcalls, they soon gathered converts and recruits.

An Army wedding at the first hall. The former Wesleyan chapel in Benhill Street was acquired by the Salvation Army in 1896, and here Robert Jobson and Maud Larkin were married on 31 August 1921. Robert's father was a member of Sutton's original tin whistle band. A new hall was built in front of the old chapel in 1926, and the corps moved to purpose-built premises forty-five years later.

The band in the Salvation Army hall, November 1958. Sutton's first brass band had tried to meet for practice in stables in Palmerston Road, but opponents had driven them out by hurling stones on to the tin roof. Here is the band that represented South London in an All-London Festival at Clapton Congress Hall many years later. Back row, left to right: Ken Still, Lars Gunnerhed, George Flatt, Malcolm Avery, Jim Edgley, Arthur Keats, Bert Smith, Bill Poole, Derrick Kennard, Tom Burberry, Fred Humphreys (with standard), Tom Hoskins, Bill Still, Michael Bissett, Les Simmonds, Les McKinnis, Bob Sharman, David Trendell, Charles Sharman, Victor Jones, Michael Justice. Front row, left to right: Norman Wallis, Ian Watkinson, Alex Purkiss, Vic Johnson, Denis Yalden, Ray Justice, Joe Hoskins, Steve South, bandmaster Reg Jobson, Vic Purkiss, Wallace Johnson, Len Justice, Rob Jobson, Robin Jones, Stan Spencer, Roy Hall, Walter Horton.

Christ church, 1900. 'The Iron Church', a temporary building in Brighton Road, was the first attempt to meet the spiritual needs of residents in the fast-growing area south of Sutton station. After some eleven years a piece of glebe land among the lavender fields was found in 1887, and the church built. The old track connecting Brighton Road and Goodenough's Lane (Langley Park Road) became Christchurch Park. The house on the left has now been replaced by Henry Hatch Court, recalling the name of an early nineteenth-century rector of St Nicholas', the parish church.

Christ church interior. This early photograph by French & Co. of Wallington shows the church before the reredos was installed. Mr N.M. Maddock recalls that the risers of the three chancel steps bore the words Faith, Hope and Charity, but since 1977 a dais has taken up this area, concealing the steps.

Chapel of the Holy Child, Christ church. Parishioners Mr and Mrs Forster gave the chapel, consecrated in 1902, in memory of two of their children who died in infancy. Paintings include 'The Christ Child and the Holy Family'. By 1984 the condition of the chapel had seriously deteriorated, and it was completely refurbished, only a small portion of the original wrought-iron railings being retained. The banner seen below is now displayed there.

GFS banner outside Christ church, c. 1924. The Girls' Friendly Society was founded within the Church of England by Mrs Mary Townsend in 1875 to give spiritual help, fellowship and recreation to young women, especially those living and working away from home. These four members (standing, left to right: -?-, Winifred Washford, Frances ?; seated: Edith Washford) did the gold thread and other embroidery on the crimson banner. Lady St George, who lived in a large house opposite the church, led the group at this time.

Congregational church, Carshalton Road. This church was built in 1889 and was demolished eighty-six years later. The brick pillar and fence mark the boundary of a small vacant lot (on which the advertising hoarding stands); beyond that was an old building with a curved wall, used as a livery stable and later as a garage. It may once have been a toll-house. To the right of the church lie the grounds of Sutton Court, a fine Georgian house that was replaced by the police station in 1909.

The Catholic church, Sutton New Town. Until 1882 Sutton's Roman Catholics faced a long journey in any direction to find a church of their own. They included a number of Irish families whose fathers came to the area for the building of the railway in 1845. A 'tin hut' on the corner of Carshalton Road and St Barnabas Road was used for worship and as a school. A decade later, the school moved to Shorts Road and the permanent Church of Our Lady of the Rosary was built. The ceiling and part of the wall decoration have since been whitened and the chancel rails removed, with some of the stone being used again for the new font, to the design of the parish priest, the Revd Father Michael Byrne.

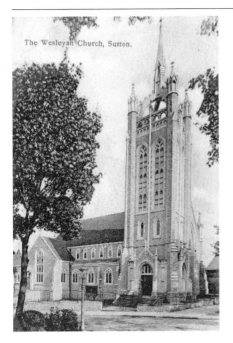

The Wesleyan Church, Sutton.

Trinity Methodist (Wesleyan) church, Cheam Road. The message on the postcard (left) sent from Lenham Road on 29 July 1908 is: 'This is the latest building in Sutton.' *Messiah*, *Elijah* and other sacred works were sung here and, not long after the end of the Second World War, I was among a small choir invited to climb the steps of the tower one chilly Christmas eve, to stand for a few minutes in the night air, singing carols. The exterior of the church has changed little in over eighty years, but the roads have altered dramatically.

TRINITY METHODIST CHURCH
CHEAM ROAD, SUTTON

MUSICAL FESTIVAL

A THANKSGIVING
for the restoration of
PEACE IN EUROPE

SUNDAY, JUNE 10th 1945 at 3 p.m.

★

Soloists
ELLISE BALSOM
ROLAND WEDDELL

★

At the Organ WALTER G. WEBBER F.R.C.O.
Conductor WILLIAM C. ANSCOMBE

The Lumley Chapel, St Dunstan's churchyard, Cheam. This small chapel, less than 21 ft wide by 27 ft long, seems to be a survival of a very early church, of Saxon and Norman date, and was restored from a ruin by the sixteenth-century Lord Lumley as a family mausoleum. His first wife was Jane Fitzalan of Nonsuch Palace and his second was Elizabeth D'Arcy. When a new church was built to the north in 1864, a number of brasses and stone memorials (some of the Fromonde family) were transferred to the chapel. These old names are remembered in the modern Darcy Road, Fromondes Road and Lumley Road, turnings off Malden Road, Cheam.

SECTION FOUR

Transport

Railway station, *c.* 1880. These buildings replaced the original wooden structure erected in 1847 to accommodate passengers for the new London, Brighton & South Coast Railway extension from West Croydon to Epsom. A service to Epsom Downs opened in 1865; part of the Brighton Road bridge over that line is on the left, behind the lamp. To the right of the main building is part of the covered exterior stairway down to the platforms, waiting- and refreshment-rooms.

Railway station from Mulgrave Road. A sermon opposing the introduction of the railway had been preached at Cheam in 1847, denouncing the shattering of Sunday peace. During the next forty years, Sutton prospered because of the wealthy businessmen who took up residence in mansions built for them; they were the early commuters. The third station, built in an attempt to keep pace with the rapidly developing network of lines, was erected by Longley's in 1883 and lasted for forty-five years.

Platforms 1 and 2, Sutton station, 1980s. The front of this goods train on the down line (Platform 2) is approaching the Bridge Road arch. Immediately beyond is the junction of the Dorking and Wimbledon lines, the latter opening in 1930. Main line trains from London to Portsmouth operated through Sutton for over a century, and the royal train bringing Queen Victoria's coffin from the Isle of Wight travelled along this line in January 1901.

Belmont railway bridge, *c.* 1910. No details are available about the drama contained in this photograph, but another near-disaster that occurred nearby has been recorded. A few years before the Second World War a truck was derailed on a curve in the line, out of sight of a fast-approaching passenger train. Quick thinking by Stan Morris, the signalman, brought the train to a halt in time to avoid a collision with the wrecked truck.

Worcester Park railway station. In April 1859 the London & South Western Railway opened the line linking Epsom and Waterloo via Wimbledon. Mansions were already being built on the former fields of Nonsuch Great Park, whose seventeenth-century custodian, Edward Somerset, fourth Earl of Worcester, gave his name to the area. New residents were early commuters from the station, and H.G. Wells described himself as one of the 'occasional literary men' who also travelled up from his home at Heatherlea, 41 The Avenue. The line was electrified in the mid-1920s.

Early motor car, Cheam Road. The horse and cart behind make an unwitting contrast with the 'shape of things to come' – one of the first horseless carriages to travel this road. What would have been the motor driver's thoughts, had he foreseen the confusion of traffic lights, direction signs and double yellow lines at this corner ninety years later, to say nothing of the other vehicles?

Milk cart and boy. Bridge's Model Dairy in Collingwood Road (formerly Balaam Road) operated for many years, appearing in local trade lists between 1909 and 1934, with slight variations in the name as son succeeded father. The churn on the cart brought milk from the dairy; the can held by the boy was for conveying milk to customers' kitchen doors; while the smaller cans suspended around the cart were for individual orders. Notice the target for a children's game chalked on the brick wall behind.

This horse pulled the cart for a Cheam greengrocer. At the end of a day's work, it was turned out in the field alongside Love Lane where little Lilian Mitchell from Quarry Lodge (*see* p. 154) would visit him.

Early trams, Carshalton and Sutton. After the first horse-drawn tram service between Thornton Heath and West Croydon started in October 1879, the introduction of electric traction at the turn of the century led to the opening of a West Croydon to Sutton link in 1906. Car no. 36 is seen (above) in Ruskin Road and (below) at the Grapes, with the High Street in the distance.

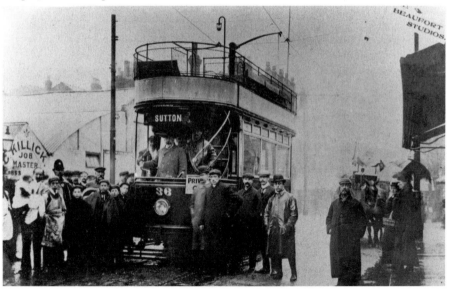

Tram terminus, Benhill Street, 1906. The West Croydon to Sutton route was one of those run by the South Metropolitan Electric Tramways & Lighting Company (SMET). Journeys terminated at the Grapes at the Sutton end, as the trams could not negotiate the sharp turn north into the High Street. A typical fare, as the board on the right shows, was 4d to Croydon. The Co-op in the middle distance served families living in the smaller homes that had been built in this part of the town. Another grocery store, Titus Ward on the south corner of Manor Lane and High Street, ran a dividend scheme to help poorer people in the hard times of the 1920s and '30s.

SMET Croydon to Sutton tram route. The company was responsible for electric light supply as well as tramways, as its full title implied. The electric light supply department of the 'South Met' had its offices and showroom at the top of the High Street, a few doors down from William Pile's corner shop, which later became Seeboard's premises. The trams' original livery was green, but for very many years it was red and white, as here. Erstwhile tram travellers will appreciate this reminder of jolting journeys with bells clanging and wheels grinding; cyclists may recall the horror of finding one's front wheel caught in the tramline.

Tram and trolleybus depot, Westmead Road. Car No. 36 (above) is on one of its early journeys eastward from Sutton. The house on the far right appears in the lower photograph as the white-walled decorator's shop with ladders outside. The depot converted from trams to trolleybuses at the end of 1935, to buses from 1959 to 1964, and has since been used by commercial enterprises. Features of the old depot remain easily identifiable.

Route 654 trolleybuses, Croydon to Sutton, 1959. The 'trolleys' replaced trams on this route in 1935, with the advantage that, unrestricted by the tracks, they could negotiate the northward bend from Benhill Avenue and go down the High Street to the Green, where they turned. A further bonus was that passengers could board and alight at the kerb, rather than risk life and limb standing in the middle of the road.

Route 164 bus in the High Street, 1935. The 164 Epsom to Morden station service, via Banstead, Belmont and Sutton, had been in operation only a few years when this street scene was photographed. The journey took approximately fifty minutes and cost 9*d*. On weekdays there were three buses per hour, with an hourly service on Sundays. Notice the positioning and parking of private cars and delivery vehicles – a thing of the past since this part of the High Street has been pedestrianized.

Granada petrol station and car park, 1958. Mrs Jean Gibbs serves petrol to the driver of a Morris Traveller on the Carshalton Road forecourt opposite Manor Park. The standard cost of a gallon of petrol in 1958 was 4s 2½d. The pump trade signs are for National Benzine (white diamond on far left) and Shell. The facility was intended for patrons of the Granada Cinema, in the background. The cinema opened in 1934 as the Plaza, with a restaurant and dance-floor upstairs. Publicity stunts included inviting patrons to stir a huge bowl of fruit-cake mixture which was then baked, slices being distributed to the audience to celebrate the cinema's anniversary. Ballet, pantomime and rock-and-roll concerts were presented as well as the usual double-feature film shows. Sutton Park House and the mouth of Throwley Way have since replaced the Granada, demolished after forty-five years.

SECTION FIVE

Schools

The County School, Throwley Road, 1908. The school was designed with the very latest facilities including a domestic science room, carpentry workshop, science laboratory and two large rooms with sliding partitions. The site was provided by Sutton Urban District Council and grants were received from Surrey County Council towards the arts and science departments. In 1920 the school expanded into Manor Park House and eight years later many of the boys transferred to the new school in Manor Lane. This old building later became the art school, and Surrey House now stands on the site.

Mr W.H. Osmond. Mr Osmond taught at the Art School, Throwley Road, and was also principal of Epsom's School of Art in Church Street from 1896 to 1930. Evening classes originally cost less than 2*d* each, for a forty-week course.

The Limes, Grove Road. Homefield Preparatory School for boys, founded in 1868 and established two years later at Sutton Park, began with forty pupils. By 1916 the number had doubled and included French, Belgian and Russian refugees from the First World War, and there were enough boarders to warrant the acquisition of the neighbouring villa, The Limes. A century after its inception, the school moved to purpose-built premises in Western Road, opened by the heroic Group Captain Douglas Bader.

Homefield v. Sutton Ladies Cricket match, 1913. Both cricket and hockey friendly matches were played annually before the First World War against the Ladies team. In 1912 Rupert Gray (back row, far left) and Charles Welford (in panama hat) became joint headmasters of this highly regarded preparatory school. When the war broke out, Mr Gray went off to fight, won the Military Cross, and returned only briefly to the school when peace was restored. Mr Welford continued as sole head until his death in 1953.

Colin Cowdrey, captain of Homefield Old Boys Eleven, June 1964. Far left is the school team captain Patrick Needham; far right, in conversation with celebrated old boy Cowdrey (now Sir Colin) is C.M.J. Chubb, who first taught at the school in 1911. Artist Graham Sutherland OM, John Ray (who became headmaster of Westminster School), and broadcaster Bob Danvers-Walker are among other distinguished former pupils. (The three Homefield photographs appear by kind permission of Peter Franklin, Homefield Old Boys Association.)

The Public Hall, Hill Road. Opened on 10 July 1879, the original hall accommodated 600 to 700 people, and a smaller building for some 200 was added eleven years later. During the First World War, while some commercial training courses were held in the Throwley Road school, others took place at the Hall. One evening my mother's shorthand lesson was interrupted by an air-raid and the girls were directed to a neighbouring building for shelter. Once there, they had a clear view of a Zeppelin bomber passing directly overhead, for their 'shelter' had a glass roof.

Manor Park House and war memorial, 1924. From about 1906 this was the 'Sutton Preparatory School for the sons of gentlemen', headmaster A.W.F. Rutty MA. Boys were accepted from the age of $6^{1}/_{2}$ up to 15 years. There was a cadet corps and fives courts, and in the 3-acre grounds cricket and football were played. The County School extended into the house in 1920, but for very many years the building was used as the public library, until its demolition in 1976. A children's play area now occupies part of the site.

The Adult School, Benhill Avenue. Wealthy bachelor Thomas Wall of Worcester Road, Sutton, whose family name has lived on through the manufacture and supply of a variety of modern foodstuffs, endowed the school as a pioneer centre for further education. It included a lecture room and hall (above). Such events as harvest suppers (below) and meetings of the Oddfellows Lodge were also held here.

West Street School. School attendance was made compulsory in 1880, but West Street had been educating boys and girls for over twenty years before that. It was supported by St Nicholas' parish church and by wealthy patrons, and children brought 'the pence' weekly as their parents' contribution, varying according to each father's income. Last lessons were given in 1968, and five years later the buildings were demolished.

Benhilton School. Four years before the Education Act of 1870 laid down that tuition should be available for every child, All Saints' church, Benhilton, set up its own school for boys and girls, close to the church and parish hall (foreground). In 1902 an infants department was added. Both school and hall were completely destroyed by enemy action in June 1944; accommodation in the south wing of Sutton West School, Crown Road, was offered to the bombed-out pupils and teachers. New buildings opened on the same site at Benhilton in 1950.

The Boys' High School, Cheam Road, 1930s. At this time the headmaster was the Revd J.B. Lawton BA (London), AKC. Some twenty years later, Mr Lawton's association with the school continued as chairman of the governors, when Mr O.J. Smith MA (Oxon) was headmaster. One distinguished former pupil is Frank Judd, now Baron Judd of Portsea.

Miss Margaret Chalmers Whyte. On 17 January 1884 a spacious house in Cheam Road opened its doors to the first eighty girls of Sutton High School. Headmistress Miss Whyte had a staff of seven, teaching a wider range of subjects than was normally found in a girls' school curriculum at that time. Pupils were sitting public examinations within fifteen months of the school's foundation, and the first university place was won in 1897.

Sutton High School orchestra, *c.* 1900. The double-bass player (far left) is Miss Jemima Fettes Duirs, a modern linguist, who succeeded Miss Whyte as headmistress in 1890. She undertook to learn the instrument when no other player could be found to complete the orchestra. Music at this time was one of the optional afternoon activities; lessons were given from 9.15 a.m. to 1.15 p.m. only.

School uniform. In 1902 the distinctive mauve touches to 'Sutton High's' uniform were confined to hatbands and ties, but thirty years later blazers and summer dresses, as worn by Nancy Frost, carried on the colour scheme.

Sutton High School, two exterior views, *c.* 1930. These snapshots recall summer schooldays before the Cheam Road buildings were altered and enlarged. Above, left to right: Edna Brookes, Moira Martin, Moira Soubrey, Vera Harrison. Below, a tennis match is in progress with unidentifiable spectators taking their ease, with the distinctive roof-line of the original school in the background.

Sutton High School, two interior views, *c.* 1930. The original hall (above), festooned with climbing ropes for its secondary use as a gymnasium, was later converted to a main hall. It is now the site of the sixth form study, and a sports hall was added in 1984. The long corridor (below) was altered to accommodate science laboratories on the left and classrooms on the right, but the whole area has since been opened up for the dining hall and kitchens. Thanks are due to Sally Cheesman for these details.

Sutton District schoolboy footballers, November 1924. The team beat Kingston and District on this occasion, but lost to Battersea the following week. Left to right: Ray, Mead, Trower, Tait, Hendon (?), Watts, Graves, Pratt, Pettitt, Bruce, Bannister. From the early 1930s, lifelong friends 'Tipper' Pratt and Claude Pettitt played (second generation) for Sutton United for many goal-full years. Tipper's father was with United from 1900, while Claude's uncle appears on p. 45 of this book with the St Barnabas football club in 1895.

The Downs School, c. 1904. The South Metropolitan Schools 'for homeless and delinquent children' had been built to the west of Brighton Road near Belmont in 1852 but were soon overcrowded, so The Downs was established in Banstead Road for girls only. In modern times it has been used as an extension of the Royal Marsden Hospital. Banstead Road was renamed Cotswold Road in the 1930s.

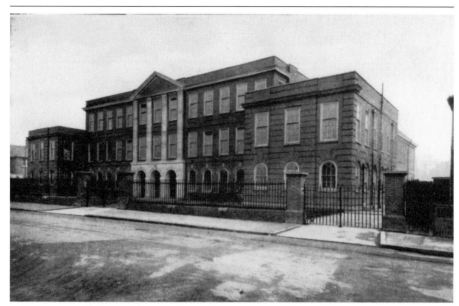

Sutton County School for boys, Manor Lane, 1928. After the school had been at Manor Park House for some eight years, headmaster Mr J.A. Cockshutt and his pupils, brought up to a complement of 500, moved a short distance north into purpose-built premises. Costing over £45,000, the new school included sixteen classrooms, an assembly hall, laboratories and an art room (below). The list of distinguished former pupils includes the Rt. Hon. Sir R.W. Goff QC, a Lord Justice of Appeal (1917–25), Gerry Worsell, a member of the national water polo team at the 1952 and 1956 Olympics (1940–48) and Professor David Bellamy, botanist, writer and broadcaster (1943–52).

Sutton East School girls' netball team, 1951. Standing, left to right: Miss Cartwright, Pauline Dean, Mary Golding, Ann Watson, Pauline Whelham, Jean Burns, Miss John. Seated, left to right: Bunny Townesend, Elsie Williamson, Sheila Albutt. There was no special school sports kit then; blouses were simply tucked into navy blue knickers.

Sutton East School, display of work, *c.* 1948. Woodwork, cooking, gardening, art and needlework are among the crafts on show. Shields representing the four school houses – Australia, Canada, New Zealand and South Africa – are on the far wall above a rail of summer dresses made by the girls. Manor Park School now occupies these buildings.

Form 3A, Sutton West County Primary School, 1948. Mr Robin Evenden has recalled, after forty-five years, the names of almost all his classmates. Back row, left to right: Mr Parfitt (headmaster), David Brewer, -?-, Ray Crane, Trevor ?, Robin Evenden, Ronnie Curteen, David Rosser, Derek Baker, Melbourne Hamer. Second row, left to right: -?-, Pat Ross, -?-, -?-, Gwen Williams, -?-, Lilian Camps, -?-, Eileen Fenner, -?-, Margaret Noel, Margaret Davies, Jean Emery, Jean Freeman, Sheila Grant, -?-, Mrs Ellis (form teacher). Seated on bench, left to right: Raine Miller, Sheila Champion, -?-, Brenda Hughes, -?-, Vera Smith, Jean Clark, Linda Chitty, -?-, Jennifer Adams, Sheila Gough, Brenda Jenkins, Dawn Parker. Seated on ground, left to right: Alan Groombridge, Ray Anscombe, Tony Matthews, Rob Starey, Peter Durham, Michael (?) Nicholson, Dai Davies, Gilbert Parkhouse, Nibbo Sheath.

Nonsuch County School girls, staff and friends. During the Second World War one of the ways senior schoolchildren could help the war effort was through spare-time farm work, and Nonsuch was one school that organized annual harvest camps. This group of girls is taking a break from potato-picking in August 1944. Standing, left to right: Camilla Huttly, Mary Goldsbrough*, Elizabeth Peck, Pamela Rose, Edna Wilson, Miss Farrant. Kneeling, left to right: Lily Valentine, Audrey Seeley, Pat Cooper, Ginnie James*. Seated, rear row, left to right: Pat Hennessy, Margaret Johnston, Rita Owen, Daphne Fletcher, Miss Henry, Molly Goodchild (obscured), Miss Finlay, Miss Linton, Dorothy Spear, Margaret Spear* (obscured). Seated, front row, left to right: Rhona Elson, Hazel Baldwin, Barbara Letchford, Ruby Smith, Celia Cockshutt, Edna Squires, Daphne Haskings. (* Denotes pupils of schools other than Nonsuch.)

St Philomena's, Pound Street. This pastoral scene behind the high walls of the girls' school was photographed by Mr David Knight Whittome, photographer to King George V, whose studios were in Sutton High Street. Carshalton House, a Queen Anne mansion, was acquired by the Daughters of the Cross in 1893 and has served as convent and school ever since.

People and Events

Children of the Tearle family, *c.* 1908. Percy, Bob, Cecil, Gladys, Dorothy, Daisy and Lilian lived with their parents in Elm Grove. There are clues in this charming backyard group to the children's pastimes, including a caged bird.

Mounted police, *c.* 1910. Constables *466* and *785* and their mounts were on the strength of W Division of the Metropolitan Police. The Carshalton Road station, opened in 1909, included a magistrate's courthouse; the small hall of the Public Hall in Hill Road had hitherto served this purpose.

Charity football match, 1912. On the night of Sunday 14 April 1912, the 45,000-ton White Star liner *Titanic* – 'the most sumptuous palace afloat' – on her maiden voyage struck an iceberg in the North Atlantic and sank in some $2\frac{1}{2}$ hours. Of the 2,224 passengers on the eleven-deck vessel, fewer than one-third were saved. Sutton United football club was only one of many groups nationwide who organized special events in aid of the dependants of those lost. In front of the seated players is a picture of the four-funnelled 'unsinkable' *Titanic*, whose commander, Captain E.J. Smith, went down with his ship.

The Sidney Arms, Collingwood Road, *c*. 1913. Well over one hundred people posed by the public house for this record of an outing of the Sidney Bottle Club. Landlord Mr E. Turnbull (hat on knees) is seated to the left of the three musicians. In white with bow ties, they are Charles and Fred Prior, with Mr Mapstone (centre), who was said to be able to play almost any musical instrument.

Sutton United football supporters, 1936. The supporters club, one of the first of its kind, was formed at a public meeting in August 1922 at the Adult School. Early activities included raising money for the main club and arranging transport to away games by coaches (then called charabancs). When United travelled to Stockton in 1936 for the third round of the FA Cup, many supporters were there to see the home team beaten. The next year, 700 supported United at Romford when the visitors won 4–3 in an epic fourth-round struggle.

Charter celebrations, 1934. Sutton's attaining borough status was celebrated with a four-day programme of twenty-six events, beginning at 10 a.m. on Wednesday 12 September when local dignitaries (above) went in horse-drawn carriages to meet the acting Lord Mayor of London, Lord Ebbisham. In Manor Park he handed the charter to Sutton's mayor, Alderman S.H. Marshall (later Sir Sidney). Later the mayor (far left below) and Lord Ebbisham (far right) attended an air display, followed by a football match, in which Sutton United defeated Queens Park Rangers 4–2, a civic ball, and a firework display and funfair. Beating the bounds, a mile-long procession of decorated vehicles, a pageant in Cheam Park, a cinema show and tea party for schoolchildren (ten thousand cups of lemonade were consumed) and a Jamboree of Youth were among other celebrations, which concluded with a civic service at Cheam parish church on Sunday the 16th.

Victory celebrations in Victoria Road, 1945. The end of the Second World War in Europe was marked everywhere with street parties. In spite of shortages and the absence of many adults, away on active service, mothers and others at home managed to organize some memorable events.

Children's victory fête in the recreation ground, 1945. The programme included a baby show 'under the supervision of the British Red Cross' judged by Drs Cotton and Murray. Above, Mayor Alderman H.J. Trickett is pictured with some of the entrants and mothers. There were also races, a tennis tournament, a Punch and Judy show, pony rides for 1*d* or 2*d*, trips on a model railway for 3*d*, and a fancy dress parade (below). (Both photographs reproduced by kind courtesy of the Croydon Advertiser Group Limited.)

Victory Parade, Gander Green Lane. Members of the voluntary services gather on Sutton United's football ground to commemorate the end of the Second World War (the same venue as for the celebrations in 1918). The three groups in the foreground are, left to right, Civil Defence (formerly Air-Raid Precautions), Women's Voluntary Service and National Fire Service (formerly Auxiliary Fire Service). The WVS contingent is led by Mrs Marjorie Barnes, Centre Organizer; the green-uniformed members, together with their young cycle-messengers, had contributed to the war effort on the home front by running canteens, emergency kitchens, clothing stores, and so on. Fifty years on they continue to serve the community as the Women's Royal Voluntary Service. In the background, standing at ease with their backs to the camera, are members of the khaki-clad Home Guard (originally the Local Defence Volunteers), Sea Rangers (a senior branch of the Girl Guides), Boy Scouts and nurses. Hairstyles and 'make do and mend' clothes of the period are interesting.

Archdeacon and Mrs Hayman, 1960s. The Revd W.S. (Sam) Hayman, with his wife and their small daughter Angela, moved into Cheam's sixteenth-century rectory in 1938 and served the parish for thirty-three years. He succeeded the late Canon Herbert Wesley Dennis. The Haymans' son Andrew was born the following year, not long before the outbreak of the Second World War, during which the rector was an air-raid warden. Enemy bombs caused casualties and destruction throughout the parish and the rectory itself was damaged more than once. The Haymans enjoyed more than twenty years in retirement.

Wartime bridesmaid, 1943. The dress was borrowed, the head-dress home-made (on hair curled with tongs heated on a gas ring), and the flowers artificial, augmented by a few from the garden, and tied with ribbons cut from another dress. Family and friends gave scarce or rationed ingredients for the wedding cake, and ersatz almond icing was made with soya flour.

Victory street party, Rosehill Park, 1945. This very large number of children from the area gathered together to celebrate the end of the war in Europe. Food rationing was at its height and nearly all non-essentials were in very short supply, but the adults organizing the party had worked wonders in producing a magnificent spread, plus paper hats and bunting. A few people even contrived fancy-dress.

A coach outing. Hector Burns and Bert Turner are among this jolly group of gentlemen from the Cross Keys public house, Vernon Road, on a day out in the 1950s.

Closure of Westmead Road bus garage, 1964. Shortly after midnight one January night, 'Tug' Wilson drove the last bus into the garage, to the singing of 'Auld Lang Syne' and West Indian calypsos. The mayor, Alderman D.P. Thomas, and other civic leaders joined the last conductor Harry Elsden and some of the 116 drivers and conductors and 22 engineers, who would be moving to jobs at other garages, for a grand farewell party in the canteen. (Published by kind courtesy of the Croydon Advertiser Group Ltd.)

Presentation to Harold Heyes, Belmont, 1976. Retiring from business after fifty years' trading as Brown's the newsagents in Station Road, Mr Heyes was honoured at a Belmont Traders' Association party on 4 February 1976 at the Conservative Club. Front row, left to right: Mrs Brenda Darby, Mr Reg Wharton, Miss Betty Heyes, Mrs Kath London, Mr Harold Heyes, Mrs Rosemary Hodges. Second row, left to right: Mrs Wharton, Ms Babs Smith, Mrs Iris Sheppard, Mrs Daphne London, Mr Alf London, Mrs Jarman, Mr Davies, Mrs Frith. Back row, left to right: Club steward, Mr Cecil Sheppard, Mr Ron Smith, Mr Tony Hodges, Mr Donald Jarman, Mr Ford, Mr John Smith, -?- from dress shop, Mrs Davies. (Thanks to Mr Heyes and Mrs Kath London for recalling these names.)

Last meeting of Sutton and Cheam Borough Council, 1965. The dying moments of a twenty-one-year-old institution were recorded by Brighton Road photographer John C. Taylor, as the mayor presided over the last council meeting before the district became a London Borough ('Borough 21'). To his left sits Alderman Andrew Letts, deputy mayor, and immediately below Mr Letts' corner of the bench is Sutton's elder statesman, with thirty-six years' service to the community, Alderman Sir Sidney Marshall. He was charter mayor and first Member of Parliament for the Sutton constituency, which was created in 1945. Far left on the bench is Archdeacon W.S. Hayman, Rector of Cheam, Chaplain to the Queen and Mayor's Chaplain. Above the mayor, part of Sutton and Cheam's coat of arms is visible, with the motto 'Serve God and be cheerful'.

SECTION SEVEN

Entertainment

Sutton music centre, 1930s. Mr Dewey and his Royal Orchestral Band provided light music at the Public Hall for early productions by the amateur dramatic club and other entertainments. His impressive music shop and piano showroom were built over the front garden of one of the original Grove Road mansions. One went there to buy records and albums of classical music, and to Landau's (now HMV) in the lower High Street for dance music and 'crooners'.

Maypole dancers. St Dunstan's schoolgirls from the local Girls' Friendly Society branch, organized by Miss Sillence and Miss Harris, danced at the opening of Cheam Sports Club. Some years later I joined the same branch, which met in the Parochial Rooms in the Broadway, and one of our activities was country dancing. We wore white blouses, flowered chintz dirndl skirts and velvet sashes.

The Public Hall, Hill Road. In 1878 the inhabitants of the fast-growing town urgently needed a central meeting place, and this 'large and commanding structure' was built at a cost of £4,000, raised by a limited liability company. Stage, screen and radio favourites like Jack Warner, Noël Coward, Leslie Howard and Gladys Young made early appearances here, and many Suttonians had their first taste of theatre-going at the Public Hall. It was demolished in 1981 and the Chancery House office block now stands on the site.

Jack Warner and Elsie and Doris Waters.
Best remembered for his portrayal of PC
George Dixon in the feature film 'The Blue
Lamp' and the television series 'Dixon of
Dock Green', Jack Warner first trod the
boards with Sutton Amateur Dramatic
Society, as Churdles Ash in *The Farmer's
Wife* in 1921. From childhood he had
played the violin in the family group, the
E.W. Waters Bijou Orchestra. His sisters
Elsie and Doris also graduated from the
group to become national entertainers 'Gert
and Daisy', Cockney charladies with
wartime morale-boosting radio
programmes.

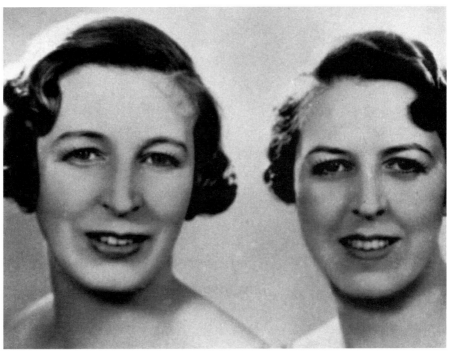

Sir Noël Coward, (1899–1973). In 1905 Mr and Mrs Arthur Coward moved with their small son Noël Pearce from Teddington to a villa in Lenham Road. Noël attended Miss Willington's local day school and at the age of six gave his first public performance, singing at an end-of-term concert. The family moved to Battersea Park in 1908. Many Coward plays have found their way into the repertoire of amateur dramatic societies: *Hay Fever*, directed by Kaye Thomas and Stephen A. Drei, was performed by the New Company of Players at Sutton Public Hall some time after the Second World War – the programme that I kept is undated.

Mabel Constanduros. Alone or in collaboration with her nephew Denis (they were next-door neighbours in Cornwall Road), Miss Constanduros wrote plays, sketches and film and radio scripts, including the 1950s 'Huggett Family' series, which starred Jack Warner and Kathleen Harrison. The inventor of an earlier radio family, the Bugginses, she played curmudgeonly Grandma Buggins, who sounded very like cartoonist Giles's 'Grandma' looks. She made her first screen appearance in a 1935 George Formby movie.

Surrey County Cinema, *c.* 1930. The first 'electric theatres' were usually converted older buildings; the Hippodrome in the former Wesleyan church in Carshalton Road is an example. The Surrey County, purpose-built in the High Street in 1920, soon deposed Sutton's smaller 'flea-pits'. It served the town's filmgoers throughout the great days of the cinema, later being renamed the Gaumont, but was demolished in 1959 to make way for retail redevelopment.

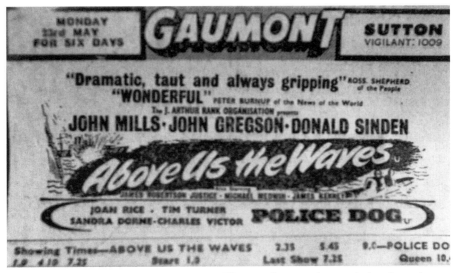

Gaumont Cinema programme, May 1955. The grand proscenium arch façade, and steps leading to vast areas of carpeted foyer and a raised refreshment corner, were enhanced by the presence of a commissionaire who seemed to have precise knowledge of the age of every schoolgirl patron, and of her eligibility to see 'A'-rated films (accompanied by an adult). This programme was doubly suitable, being all-British and all-'U' (admission to all age groups).

The Joan Watts School of Dancing, 22 May 1936. All forty-eight pupils took part in a display of 'dance, ballet and mime' in aid of Carshalton Hospital. Six of the older girls held membership of the Royal Academy of Dancing, and at that time one (Jean Wigglesworth) was a scholar of the Academy. Classes were held at 99 Carshalton Park Road and 23 Beynon Parade. The girls' dresses for this finale were of apple-green satin and net, with candy-pink ribbons. Dancers included Angela Appleby, Daphne Arnott, Peter and Wendy Barratt, Sheila Bell, Josie Brain, Jean Brooke, Sheila Christmas, Rosemary Clarke, Pamela Comber, Betty Cooke, Annette Davies, Maureen Edwards,

Derek Ellis, Philippa Foreshew, Jean Francis, Heather and Leslie Funnell, Hazel Gay, Pat Geldart, Babs Gleeson, Beryl Godfrey, Beryl Grover, Jean Hancock, Denise Heady, Jenifer Healey, Pat Hennessy, Daphne Hews, Heather Hitchcock, Mary Johnston, Marion Larcombe, Andree and Keith Lawson, Sheila Lee, Maureen Leese, Ann McEwing, Daphne Pearce, Margaret Phillips, Barbara Reeder, Pamela Rook, Audrey Seller, Dorothy Sockle, Ann Strathman, Pat Teasdale, Joan Tucker, Jean Wigglesworth, Rosemary Williams and Mary Woolveridge. Miss Watts is on the left, holding the bouquet.

Jimmy Hanley (1918–70). Jimmy lived for some time in the Sutton Common Road area and was a popular 'opener' of local fetes and other events. As a child he appeared on stage in *White Horse Inn*, and he made his first film, *Little Friend* (scriptwriters included Margaret Kennedy and Christopher Isherwood), in 1934. His last film role was in a Hammer production *The Lost Continent* thirty-four years later, but he is probably best remembered as the young police constable in the 1949 Ealing Films success *The Blue Lamp*, and for the radio and television programmes to which he turned his talents before his untimely death.

René Ray (1911–93). Several older Suttonians have passed on their recollections of seeing René Ray (Irene Creese) as a local youngster, cycling around the town. She made her first film appearance at the age of 19 in *Young Woodley* and her last almost thirty years later in *Vicious Circle*, a Francis Durbridge thriller starring John Mills. She took supporting roles in many British pictures including *The Good Die Young*, made in 1954 and frequently shown on modern television.

The Little Soldier, May 1937. Coronation fever gripped the country that year, and the Joan Watts School of Dancing was no exception. The finale of their 'Dancing Matinée', in which all seventy-three pupils took part, was set to the music of *Red, White and Blue*. The military-style hats were purchased, but our mothers made the satin jackets (with gold braid) and tarlatan tutus. This snapshot was taken in the back garden of 36 Malden Road, Cheam, with the spire of St Dunstan's church in the background.

St Anthony's Hospital garden party. In June 1963 the annual fund-raising garden party was attended by David Jacobs, television and radio star. Accompanied by the sister superior, Sr Mary Perpetua, and surrounded by nurses, patients and visitors, he signed autographs. (Published by kind courtesy of the Croydon Advertiser Group Ltd.)

St Mary's Children's Home, Sandy Lane, Cheam. At Christmas 1965 the Mayoress of Sutton and Cheam, former Nonsuch County School pupil Mrs Margaret Vaughan (née Thomas), visited the home for the nativity play. The home had opened with great ceremony on 6 November 1914. It closed in 1968, and Chesham Close has since been developed on the site. (Published by kind courtesy of the Croydon Advertiser Group Ltd.)

Babes in the Wood, 1971. In the pantomime, staged at Carshalton Hall, Dave Knight appeared as the dame, with support from members of the Margaret Dixon School of Dancing, Cheam Road, Sutton. Principal singer was Marilyn Hill Smith, then aged nineteen. Another ex-Nonsuch School pupil, she studied at the Guildhall School of Music before engagements with the English National Opera, Royal Opera, and other companies.

SECTION EIGHT

Sports and Hobbies

Entrance to recreation ground, Collingwood Road. Balaam Lane, a track which later became Collingwood Road, ran due east of and parallel with the old parish boundary. Sutton United football club has played home games here since 1919. The Sutton to Wimbledon railway line passes on the south side of the ground and footpaths lead through to Gander Green Lane.

Sutton United football club, Christmas morning, 1908. Ten years after its formation, the club staged a 'Past v. Present' game. Back row, left to right: G. Legg, H. Grover, G. Wood, J. Harris, F. Wood, -?-, G. Wood, A. Rendell, G. Simmonds, F. Seabrook. Second row: A. Harris, -?-, W. Harding, H. Turner, C. Muddle, S. Collins, W. Sansum (keeper), C. Leeding, W. Gough, J.B. Wicking (captain), H. Kirby, F. Quick, W. Scott. Third row (on bench): R. King, R. Broad, J.A. Quick, J.W. Worker ('Bill'), W. Wood, W. Turner, E.J. Quick ('Jimmy'), J. Wyatt, C. Clover. Fourth row (on ground): E. Shrubsole, F. Trower, A. Poulter, Caleb Smith (keeper), B. Taylor, H. Moore. Shadowy figures in the background suggest that the club had not entirely solved their old problem of non-paying spectators. During the 1940–41 season, a similar game was played in an effort to keep local interest alive during the difficult days of war.

The Public Baths, Throwley Road. The baths, 75 ft long and 30 ft wide and containing some 72,000 gallons of water, were built by the local authority at a cost of nearly £7,000, and opened in April 1903. They offered both swimming and bathing facilities, in the days when few homes had bathrooms. In right-angled Throwley Road, from the corner of the High Street, the municipal offices, fire station, art school, public baths, 'top' of the arcade, YWCA and Gliderdrome roller-skating rink (said to be the largest in England) made a familiar sweep of frontages till Throwley Way was developed with Surrey House and Times House; only the arcade has survived.

Sutton United football club, 1934–5. In this season, Dick Tarrant played for Ireland, Bill Shepherd and Claude Pettitt were selected for Association, County and Athenian League representative games, Ralph Carr and Tommy Delventhal for League games, and 'Tipper' Pratt for Surrey. Archie Mason went on to become team trainer in the 1945–6 season, and in 1947–8 Ralph Carr played for England against France, and was in the Olympic soccer squad. Back row, left to right: G. Luxford, H. Pratt, R. Carr, A. Ready, W.A. Shepherd, A.T. Mason. Front row: R. Tarrant, B. Solly, C. Pettitt (captain), H.J. Delventhal, C. Williams. My uncle Henley 'Tubby' Washford, after several appearances for Crystal Palace, played a number of times for United in this season, including a game at centre forward on 11 January 1935, when Tarrant was not available.

Sutton West County Primary Junior Mixed School cricket team, 1949. Standing, left to right: Mr Kelsey (cricket master), Gordon Bamber, Steve Dunwoody, Brian Healey, Ray Crane, David Freeman, Melbourne Hamer. Seated, left to right: David Brewer, Tony Hoare, Alan Groombridge, Robin Evenden, Rob Starey, Michael Docherty, Tony Matthews. Robin says he was made captain because he owned long white flannel trousers, so looked the part. Sutton West was formerly known as Crown Road schools, and Robin's father Arthur 'Toffee' Evenden and his mother Olive (née Tickner) were pupils there in the 1920s when Mr W.J. Roberts was headmaster.

Amateur radio report cards. The G6 series call (above) was issued between 1921 and 1939 but withheld throughout the Second World War for reasons of security. The Egmont Road transmitter/receiver in 1946 used a 15 ft long indoor antenna, signified by ⅛ on the card, since a complete long wire for 3 Mhz frequency was 120 ft. The G2 three-letter call signs (below) were issued as an experimental licence before the Second World War, for use in the building of home-made equipment, transmitting for test purposes only. Obtaining a full licence involved passing a Morse Code test. The reverse of the card gives details of a club contest run by *Shortwave Magazine*, held in November 1952. (Thanks to Neil Allchin LCGI RA, G 7 PGZ of Seaford, East Sussex.)

Sutton Water Company football team, 1949–50. The water company has for many years had its own extensive sports ground off Gander Green Lane. Back row, left to right: Ken Woodfield, -?-, R. Matthews, ? Shurley, ? Ladbrook, Ted Gray, Bill Gray, ? Casalton. Front row, left to right: Ginger ?, ? Bennett, Joe Williams, ? Brown, F. Gaby, ? Bones.

Salvation Army band soccer team, 1955. The Sutton band travelled extensively within the United Kingdom and Europe, appearing at national congresses and on television, as well as playing for radio, hospitals, prisons, old people's homes, carol concerts and the like. While on a visit to Hereford in 1955, Sutton formed a soccer team to play against a side from the home corps – and won.

Speedway riders Barry Briggs and Ronnie Moore. When Wimbledon Speedway resumed after the Second World War, promoter Ronnie Greene set about rebuilding his side with former riders augmented by a stable of new discoveries. In 1952 New Zealanders Barry, then aged 17, and Ronnie (aged 19 and already a star of 'the Dons'), together with fellow-riders Geoff Marden and Trevor Redmond, lodged at a house in Duke of Edinburgh Road, Sutton. At one stage Barry rode for New Cross, hence his team badge in this picture. Between them, he and Ronnie won the world championship six times. (Photograph by courtesy of *Vintage Speedway Magazine*.)

SECTION NINE

Towards Carshalton

Carshalton Road looking east, *c.* 1910. The road was first made up from a track through fields in 1755, when it acquired a toll-house through the Turnpike Acts. The 'round house' existed opposite Manor Park until comparatively recent times. Sutton New Town was developed along this road in the mid-nineteenth century; built over a layer of Thanet sand, there were no problems in finding sources of fresh water. Greyhound Road and Vernon Road grew from a parallel track through fields.

Manor Park. Though a strip of ground on the west side of the park was lost when Throwley Way was developed for the new town centre, many features in these postcard views remain today. The fountain is still there, as are some of the old trees by the path leading to Greyhound Road. There was an underground public air-raid shelter in one corner during the Second World War, and open-air concerts were given here.

Remembrance Day at the war memorial, 1963. The mayor of Sutton, Alderman D.P. Thomas, lays a wreath on behalf of the borough, while representatives of local organizations await their turn to pay their respects to the war dead. In the background is Carshalton Road with the row of shops (left) and Granada Cinema filling station and Congregational church (right), swept away in the revised road layout of the town centre plan revealed in January 1964. (Published by kind permission of the Croydon Advertiser Group Ltd.)

The Lagoon, Carshalton Road. Shops numbered 48 to 58 were built into the steep northern slope of the old pit, which lay between Carshalton Road and Sutton Court Road. Their rear view would have been an alarming revelation to customers. During the water company's occupation, the pit held chalk sludge, separated off in the purifying process. The iron safety railings and bushes in Carshalton Road have survived, and modern retail warehouses, reached via Chalk Pit Way, now occupy the low ground.

Sutton and Cheam Water Company. The company was founded with capital of £8,000 in 1863, under the Waterworks Clauses Act, with the intention of piping a regular supply to every home in the town. By 1900, it had laid 142 miles of mains. Harry Gillis (left) was water inspector in 1910. Mr W. Mercer and Mr C. Windsor in the company's smithy (below) would have forged, repaired and welded machinery and equipment for the waterworks and also acted as farriers, as at that time horses were used for the carting and heavy draught work later undertaken by motor vehicles. A blacksmith from almost a century earlier lies in the parish churchyard; William Juniper's epitaph begins, 'My sledge and hammer lie declined, My bellows too have lost their wind. . . .'

The Elms, Carshalton Road. The first land acquired by the water company included an early Victorian house, The Elms (above), used as the waterworks' offices, and cottages (below). Two pillars, once marking the entrance to the house and still bearing its name, have survived adjacent to the main road above the Turnpike Lane development.

Constructing early waterworks, *c*. 1900. Less than twenty years after the founding of the water company, a local guidebook reported that 'to cope with the enormously increasing demands upon the company, additional and more powerful engines and machinery are now being erected, which will materially add to the hitherto efficient services rendered to customers'. The Elms is in the background of the upper photograph; the engine house (below) stood near the north-east corner of the site, bounded by Jenny Lind Road and the track which became Greyhound Road.

Water Company tanks, 1930s. There was an early reservoir on Banstead Downs (p. 142), while the one at the corner of Brighton Road and Ventnor Road had good enough acoustics for the country's leading viola player Lionel Tertis (a Belmont resident and First World War special constable) to practise while guarding it. During the Second World War it was feared that the wide blue waters of the Carshalton Road tanks (above) would be a landmark and target for enemy aircraft. A covering supported on battens (below) camouflaged them to resemble a ploughed field when seen from the air.

The lavender fields. Little more than a century ago, Sutton, Carshalton and Wallington stood as separate communities amid field after field of lavender. The flowers were gathered and sent to distilleries at Mitcham for use in perfumes and lotions. An old map of the district shows that mint was also grown in quantity, and a distillery for peppermint flavourings stood near Westmead Road.

Langley Park Road, looking north from The Crossways, 1929. This is the newer part of the road, extended after the Highfields Estate was opened up for residential building in 1905, from the former Goodenoughs Lane leading south from Carshalton Road. During the summer of 1893 writer H.G. Wells and his first wife Isobel lived in this road at 4 Cumnor Villas. While there, he wrote one of his 'chatty articles', 'Out Banstead Way', for the *Pall Mall Gazette*.

The Jenny Lind Inn, *c.* 1918. The 'Swedish nightingale', prima donna Jenny Lind, was a sensation on her visits to the London opera scene in Victorian times. Staying with friends in Sutton, she sang from the balcony of the inn to crowds gathered in the street below. Her portrait now hangs in the bar.

The Ponds, looking south-east, 1905. For more than thirty years, until a station was built in Pound Street for the volunteer fire brigade, their pump was kept in a small room behind the door in the corner of the churchyard wall. To the right of the door, a circular railing in the road encloses Anne Boleyn's well which was yet another water source in an area of several ponds, streams and springs. The old white house, with even older elements absorbed by it, was known as Queen's Well House, and was replaced in the mid-1960s by flats for elderly people.

Water Tower and Margaret's Pool, West Street, 1905. Art critic and social reformer John Ruskin knew this area from childhood. In about 1870 he found the spring had declined into a rubbish dump, so he arranged for its purifying and re-stocking with fish and flowers in memory of his mother, whose name it still bears. The tower across the road worked a very early system of piped water to Carshalton House; its plunge bath with Delft tiles is now open as part of Sutton's Heritage Service.

Westcroft at the junction with Acre Lane. This former mill area, whose open canal once ran beside the High Street (p. 129), now gives access to the borough's sports and leisure centre, opened in 1971.

The Ponds, looking south-west, 1910. The posts with chain strung across the water mark the course of the ancient ford, used by carts and carriages until the bridge was built at the beginning of the nineteenth century. On the left is the old Greyhound Inn and on the right, overlooking the pond, is Honeywood, recently refurbished and open to the public as Sutton's Heritage Centre. Originally comprising a small millhouse and the sixteenth-century Wandle Cottage, it was rebuilt in late Victorian times. The quality of this postcard is remarkably fine, especially in the details of flowers and shrubs, and the reflections.

The war memorial, 1920s. After the First World War part of the garden (seen on p. 127) was paved and railed off to make an impressive setting for Carshalton's own cenotaph at the very edge of the water. Honeywood is again in the background.

The High Street, leading west, 1935. In the small area between the kerb and the churchyard wall are four objects of nostalgia. The two 'trade-bikes', ridden by delivery boys with packages stacked in the deep baskets on the front, belong to the butcher's shop on that corner, once Mr Woodman's. The edge of a tiled roof, supported by posts, is part of a shelter where meat was suspended on display. Behind is a blue Metropolitan Police box with lamp on the roof and doors to the emergency telephone and first aid kit.

High Street from Westcroft, *c.* 1910. So much has changed since this view was photographed that it is necessary to orientate by the tower of All Saints' parish church in the middle distance. By the 1920s the stream on the left, the remains of an eighteenth-century canal serving a mill converting tobacco into snuff, had a railing to guard it; by the Second World War it had been piped underground. Buildings on both sides of the road hereabouts were damaged in air-raids in the early 1940s.

The Grove, 1940s. Only minutes from the High Street, which has seen so much change in eighty years, these quiet gardens have altered very little since this postcard was sent half a century ago. The paths follow the same courses, some trees have survived, and the Wandle flows as before.

Parks in Carshalton. The town is well endowed with open spaces, and the Westcroft Sports and Leisure Centre was added to its recreational facilities in 1971. There is an abundance of natural water in the area – streams, ponds and weirs – which give a rural atmosphere to this part of the London Borough of Sutton.

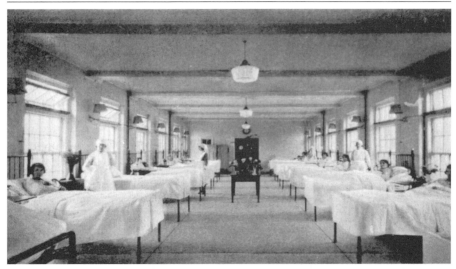

The War Memorial Hospital and Carshalton Park. Carshalton Cottage Hospital was founded in Rochester Road in 1899, and enlarged ten years later. It had moved for greater space to the Park by 1924 but even there required enlargement to sixty beds by 1930. An anonymous endowment enabled a separate nurses' home to be built. Across the road are views into the old deer park enclosed by magnificent railings, a reminder of the seventeenth-century home of the lords of the manor.

The Hack Bridge, 1904. Housing and industrial estates now cover much of the land around the Wandle (including the old kennels and pets' cemetery by the railway line). Barely a quarter of a mile from the London road, the river is still a reminder of a gentler way of life when mills in the area were producing an assortment of commodities including corn, calico, snuff, leather and peppermint.

SECTION TEN

Towards Belmont

Brighton Road and Mulgrave Road. Though horse-drawn cabs were still on the rank outside the new (1928) railway station, this postcard is considerably older. Estate agents' offices were strategically placed to attract rail travellers arriving in search of homes; as well as Dixon's in the centre, Morgan, Baines & Clark had premises immediately opposite the station. Their official postal address was 'opposite the station'. The water trough, around which the Salvation Army band sometimes played, must have been a welcome sight for horses that had climbed the Cock Hill.

Home Guard unit of Joint Electricity Authority, Wellesley Road. By 1932 the town's electricity supply was in the hands of the JEA; when war broke out seven years later, the company formed its own unit of Local Defence Volunteers, later renamed the Home Guard, responsible for the security of this essential service. The group includes my father (Corporal) Ernie Hennessy (second from right), then an electrician plumber/jointer, and his jointer's mate, Jack Laws (third from right). The building behind them remains little changed, though most of the assorted meeting huts in Wellesley Road have gone, together with the temperance society coffee stall that once stood on the north corner of Brighton Road.

Opposite top: Aerial view of railway station area, 1964. This is the Sutton that we knew before the development of the new town centre and one-way traffic scheme. From top to bottom of the photograph runs Brighton Road, curving slightly on its way past Cedar Road towards Belmont. Mulgrave Road comes in diagonally from the bottom left-hand corner, joining Brighton Road opposite the railway station. Towards the top right-hand corner is Carshalton Road with the war memorial in Manor Park. Great changes were to come near the parish church (top left) to accommodate St Nicholas Way. (Published by kind courtesy of the Croydon Advertiser Group Ltd.)

Opposite: Brighton Road, looking north towards Cedar Road. The old way south from the Cock Hotel to Banstead Downs was, until improvements were made under the Turnpike Acts, a desolate track across uninhabited rough land. The section shown here was particularly vile, frequently little more than a stinking bog, known locally as 'the slough'. The advent of the railway and the water company encouraged building of family homes in this south Sutton area; in the decade 1870 to 1880, the number of houses increased six-fold.

Cedar Road, 1905. The Cedars, a mansion with extensive grounds on the east side of Brighton Road, was occupied in 1880 by Mr Willan. The trees from which it took its name were then some two hundred years old; one survived to be featured in the 1980 redevelopment of The Quadrant. As soon as the water company was able to supply water to properties to the south, a network of roads built up in that direction.

Albion Road, 1905. Because so many professional men took up residence in the south Sutton mansions (handy for the trains), the area was nicknamed 'New Harley Street' by local people. Many of the Victorian houses have now been demolished or converted, but the later Onyx Property development on the Sutton Farm estate, nearer Belmont, remains relatively unaltered.

New housing south of the railway station, *c.* 1870. Another of the Victorian developments in Sutton's 'stockbroker belt', Cavendish Road (above) was once exclusive enough to be closed off from Brighton Road by a gate. The small chalet-style house on the north corner would have been the gatekeeper's lodge. Hillcrest (below), set in its own orchard with protective whitening of the fruit tree trunks, was typical of the large detached houses built throughout the new estates between Brighton Road and the old Goodenoughs Lane, renamed Langley Park Road.

Looking north at the junction with Christchurch Park. Near this corner the iron church of Christchurch opened in 1876, to serve the needs of the new community developing to the south of the railway station. The imposing villas, built at about the same time for wealthy families, have all been demolished but many of the trees planted along the road have survived. A plaque on the corner near the cart commemorates the work of George Edgar Alcock in campaigning to save the trees.

The California Hotel, Brighton Road, looking north. The bushes on the left mark the boundary of land running west to the railway line, not built on until the 1940s era of pre-fabricated houses. Today Hulverstone Close and a network of other closes occupy the site. The inn sign showed to advantage opposite the California, which was named in honour of the gold-mining connections of its founder, John Gibbons.

The California Hotel, interior, 1943. Mr Arthur Perrin and Mr G. Carr are seated at the centre table in the bar, which was destroyed later in the Second World War when the public house received a direct hit from an enemy bomb. What remained of the old building was repaired and continued to function until the site was redeveloped as the Belmont Carvery.

Near Belmont railway station, *c.* 1920. Until the middle of the nineteenth century, the only substantial building along the lonely turnpike road south to Banstead Downs was Little Hell, a notorious inn. After the South Metropolitan schools, the third Middlesex County Lunatic Asylum (with workers' cottages in Downs Road) and the station were built, a few shops (above) came to serve the community. Linking the station and the asylum, the track (below) enabled building materials to be brought to the site in horse-drawn wagons. After the asylum opened in March 1877 inmates' visitors had to walk up the track from the station.

The village, looking east towards the Downs, 1908. William Henry Brain, stationer, issued a set of tinted postcards at this time which show us how little Belmont's shops and houses have changed in more than eighty years. In 1928 an iron footbridge, formerly at Folkestone Junction, was installed immediately to the north of the road bridge for the convenience of rail users. In the early 1990s the group of homes called Common Side was built in the extreme northern corner of the Downs.

Station Road, looking west, 1920s. This is the view from the road bridge in the photograph above. Dense iron railings have replaced the flimsy wooden fence separating the footpath from the steep grass bank of Station Approach. Huggett's garage had yet to be built on the empty site behind the lamppost, but Barclays Bank is already installed in its cabin-like premises on the opposite corner.

Band of Hope outing to the Downs, *c.* 1904. The Band of Hope, founded in around 1847, was a temperance organization for young people. Behind this well-dressed group is the wall of the reservoir which served customers in the south of Sutton Water Company's area. Ironically, in the company's centenary year, 1963, its first failure to maintain a supply occurred when, one Tuesday in June, the evening watering of gardens ran this small reservoir dry.

A path across the Downs, 1930. Rural postcard scenes like this were always popular with casual visitors, as reminders of their 'day out'. Coming by omnibus or train from London, they felt that even the very edge of the Downs was 'the countryside'. Many went no further than the grass beside Belmont bus terminus to picnic, gather flowers and play cricket.

SECTION ELEVEN
Towards Cheam

From Robin Hood Lane, looking east. This postcard view, sent only weeks before the outbreak of the First World War in 1914, gives glimpses of buildings near the Cock Hotel in the High Street. Through the trees behind the cyclist the old variety theatre is glimpsed. In the 1920s it was converted to show silent films, and completed its entertaining career as the three-tier Curzon Cinema.

By Trinity church looking west. Though a few bushes and trees have survived, few people today would believe that Cheam Road ever presented this idyllic, sylvan scene. The volume and speed of modern traffic dictated the removal of the handy steps cut in the boundary walls. A commentary on changing attitudes and customs in eighty years is contained in the message on this postcard, sent from Balham in August 1911: 'Have just returned from a tramp to Sutton – phew.' This is a round trip of 12 miles.

From Church Road (St Nicholas Way), looking west, 1905. This is a similar view to the last, with the red brick wall on the far corner of Robin Hood Lane in the middle distance. This postcard bears a comment on the weather: 'Talk about fogs, it is so thick I can't find my way about.' 'Kitty' then enthuses over the greenery and paths: 'You would often get knocked down if it wasn't for them.' (She had previously lived in rural Suffolk.)

Grove Road and post office, 1909. The car is parked outside the new post office, with its classical façade. In 1880, when Sutton's population had just reached the 10,000 mark, the head post office was at 6 High Street (one of the buildings on the left in the lower photograph on p. 21) with sub-offices in Lind Road and Upper High Street. There were fifteen posting boxes within the area, four deliveries per day and 'five bags despatched to London daily'.

Victory parade, Grove Road, 1945. District Warden David Philip Thomas is at the head of the detachment of Civil Defence (Air-Raid Precautions) personnel, passing the saluting base set up outside Wilson's Restaurant. Mr Thomas became a borough councillor in 1947 and earned the nickname 'Mr Road Safety' for his work in that field. He was mayor of Sutton in 1957–8, 1963–4 and 1964–5.

Grove Road, looking towards the High Street. The same parade of shops appears above; they include McCabe, the optician's, Noel Lesley, the furrier, the Christian Science reading room and the motor showrooms on the corner. The pillarbox and telephone kiosks remind me that a temporary post office was set up here in 1952 while the main office on the other side of Grove Road was being rebuilt.

The dogs of Camborne Road. Smuttie (above) belonged to the Lovell family of Southview. He was enjoying country life when this snapshot was taken in the summer of 1910, but his people were unsure how he would react when they moved to a London flat in the autumn. No name is given for the terrier at the gate of Pentamar (below), where the Metcalf family lived; one wonders if the two dogs ever met, and how kindly they took to each other. Camborne Road has retained few of the prosperous villas from this era but one which has survived is no. 16, where artist Graham Sutherland lived as a boy attending Homefield School (p. 69).

Grange Road, 1907. The Grange stood in its own extensive grounds to the south of Mulgrave Road, until they were developed for housing when the area became fashionable. Politician Sir John Anderson was one distinguished resident; as Home Secretary at the outbreak of the Second World War, he gave his name to corrugated metal shelters, distributed to families for protection in the event of enemy air raids.

Ravenstor, Grange Road. The children are Billy Tagg and Janet Benmore, playing in the garden on 10 May 1912. Very few of the older houses remain and this is one I have not been able to find, in spite of its many distinctive features.

Robin Hood Lane, *c.* 1905. This road, leading to the inn (below) after which it is named, once turned directly north off Cheam Road, but redevelopment of the area has obliterated the old brick walls and venerable trees and narrowed the opening. The line of Camden Road on the left and the twitten on the right, which runs alongside St Nicholas rectory, marks the original boundary track between two parishes. Love Lane, at the Cheam end, runs close to St Dunstan's church.

Brock's Crystal Palace fireworks, Gander Green Lane. C.T. Brock & Company's factory moved to Cheam at the turn of the century, and there continued the peacetime manufacture of rockets and firecrackers till 1934. During the First World War the works became a munitions factory. A Portland stone monument, still to be seen in Sutton Cemetery, records the deaths of employees in explosions while on duty. An estate of some 1,600 houses was built on the factory site, after Brock's left the district.

Bore holes, Gander Green Lane. In December 1922 experimental drillings were made on water company land at Cheam, in the quest for further water sources to satisfy the demands of an ever-growing population.

Steam engines at Gander Green Lane, 1922. A small works was established at Woodmansterne in 1903, and the supply of water was developed rapidly at the Gander Green Lane site from 1921. A further station at Nork was opened in 1927 but disposed of during the Second World War. There is also a long-established reservoir off Langley Park Road.

The Bourne, Love Lane, looking north-east. Known locally as 'Boney Hole', the bourne would occasionally rise through the Thanet sand to form a small temporary lake. The water company later built a pumping station nearby to obviate this, so that the walk between Cheam and Sutton along Love Lane (railed off on the right) was less picturesque, but drier.

Gander Green Lane. The water company's imposing new buildings opened in 1921, and its modern high-tech premises are on the same site. Every account of the history and development of Sutton pays warm tribute to the invaluable part played by the company in opening up hitherto uninhabitable land by extending the water supply. (With grateful acknowledgement of the courtesy of Mr C.T. Loring, managing director of Sutton District Water plc, for permitting me to use sixteen photographs from the archives.)

The Quarry, 1920s. Home of Mr and Mrs Seear, the house stood in extensive grounds to the north of Cheam Street, and was reached by a long drive with a concealed entrance, where Quarry Park Road now runs parallel with the by-pass. The present day sunken garden at this spot marks the site of the old quarry from which the house took its name. Seven acres of open land were bequeathed to the borough and made into Seears Park, now bounded by Love Lane, the by-pass and the water company's grounds. The snow-wading dog was called Spot.

Quarry Lodge, 1926. The lodge, occupied at this time by Mr and Mrs Mitchell and daughter Lilian, stood close to the front gates of The Quarry, opening directly on to Cheam Street (now Cheam Road, the A232). The road to Sutton ran downhill for some distance from this point, lined with trees and fences. The introduction of the by-pass (St Dunstan's Hill), soon after this snapshot was taken, heralded great changes to the area as roads were widened and desirable residences developed.

Love Lane, looking west towards the by-pass, 1930. The new road was used to avoid Belmont and Sutton. On some Derby days in the early 1930s King George V and Queen Mary travelled by car to Epsom Downs along the new road, and Cheamites would wait patiently on this corner for a brief glimpse. The old king always doffed his hat in acknowledgement of the cheers. This postcard was published by Mrs Rowe, whose sweet shop on the corner of Cheam Broadway and Park Lane will be fondly remembered by many.

THE OLD COTTAGE   CHEAM

Malden Road, looking north, 1926. This postcard bears the impressed address of The Rectory, Cheam, and a message of thanks for birthday greetings from the rector himself, Canon Wesley Dennis. In order to widen the road, thereafter known as the Broadway, the old cottage (then a cycle repair shop) was moved some yards north and re-opened as council rent offices. The very inky franking which defaced the postcard reads 'British goods are best'.

Railway arch, Sandy Lane, 1913. The single-storey building and wall (far left) are part of The Cold Blow, a house built for Mr Edward Boniface, the owner of Cheam Brewery and said, like others in the village, to contain relics of King Henry VIII's Nonsuch Palace. The house stands on the corner of Peach's Close, named after the Revd Henry Peach BD, rector of St Dunstan's from 1780 to 1813. The church spire can be seen in the distance (right).

Open-air service, Malden Road. These two snapshots, marked 1919, show men, women and children congregating on open ground on the south corner of Malden Road and Lumley Road. In the background (above) are the spire of St Dunstan's church and the end wall of 40 Malden Road. Below, the houses are on the north side of Lumley Road, with the tall chimney of Cheam brickworks in the distance, and the trees at the top of the Church Hill (far right). The date, the group of clergy and the presence of soldiers in the crowd suggest this may be a First World War peace day ceremony, or armistice commemoration.

The Drive, Nonsuch Mansion, 1904. Captain W.R.G. Farmer inherited the estate in 1860 from his father, who had enhanced the gardens, already famous for their lilacs and magnificent trees, by introducing exotic plants such as ericas, azaleas and orchids. In the following seventy-six years of the family's ownership, the Georgian mansion became a popular house-party venue, with an indoor staff of twelve, including a liveried butler and footmen, as well as gardeners and farm-workers, a coachman and grooms. Along this drive, past the sixteenth-century flint and chalk chequered wall, came the carriages of the rich and famous, royalty and aristocracy. Shortly before the Second World War the estate was acquired by the adjacent local authorities and became the responsibility of a joint management committee. In 1991, faced with the possibility of the mansion and park becoming part of a golf course, a group of enthusiasts formed the Friends of Nonsuch to promote the restoration of the property. Already the service wing is open for school visits, and a rare stained glass window awaits reconstruction.

The barn church, Gander Green Lane, *c.* 1935. Dedicated to St Alban, this unusual church was created from parts of the dismantled farmhouse and barns of Cheam Court, one of the farms of the Tudor Nonsuch Palace. The materials were bought by the rector and churchwardens of St Dunstan's parish church in 1929, when the estate was sold for demolition and redevelopment. A carved inscription tells the congregation: 'The glories of Nonsuch have passed away, but the beams of these humble buildings remain, and are now around you.'

Poplar Road, *c.* 1935. On the extreme north of the London Borough of Sutton, where Sutton Common Road meets Stonecot Hill, a small group of interlinked roads have the names of trees. This quiet scene contains many reminders of childhood just before the Second World War, not least the greengrocer's horse and cart. Most shops had their own delivery vehicles, but some traders conducted business in the streets, having no other premises.

St Anthony's Hospital, North Cheam. The Daughters of the Cross founded the hospital in 1904 in premises that were formerly the Lord Nelson coaching inn. New buildings opened in time to accommodate soldiers wounded in the First World War. A sanatorium was also established which received patients for treatment until 1934. In that year I was in the hospital children's ward for a short time, and have never forgotten the loving care given by nuns and nurses alike. A further new hospital opened in 1975.

Acknowledgements

Though based on the photographs and postcards of my home area, collected nostalgically over a thirty-year period of exile from Surrey, this book has been greatly enhanced by advice, reminiscences or the loan of pictures, all warmly appreciated, from:

Emma Sweetman (Appeals Department, Girls Friendly Society & Townsend Fellowship) • Mrs Pink (Headmaster's secretary, Sutton Grammar School for Boys) • the Revd P. Thompson (St Barnabas Church) • Revd Fr M. Byrne (Our Lady of the Rosary Catholic Church) • Deaconess Marian Randall (Christ Church) • Mr Reg Jobson (Salvation Army) • Mrs V. Barkey (Headmistress, Nonsuch High School for Girls) and members of the Old Girls' Association, in particular Mrs Maureen Adamson (Chairman) • Mrs Barbara Edser
Mr John Bristoll • Mr Tony Michelle (British Film Institute)
Mrs Jean Gibbs and Mr Graham Gibbs • the Chairman and all at Sutton United Football Club, in particular Mrs Sylvia Holland, Mr Ralph Carr and Mr Tipper Pratt • Mr Morris Andrews • Mrs Audrey Banham
Mrs Lilian Curd • Mrs Sylvia and Mr Laurence Curtis
Mrs Margaret Vaughan • Mr and Mrs Laurie Henwood • the staff of the Surrey County Record Office • Lewes and Seaford Public Libraries, East Sussex
Mr Malcolm Spence of Sutton Cemetery • Suzanne Tagg (Science Museum) and a special mention as usual for my friend, chauffeur and sounding-board Miss Audrey Seeley.

Books consulted in checking of facts and figures included *Jack of all Trades* by Jack Warner; *The Quest for Nonsuch* by John Dent; *West Croydon to Epsom* by Vic Mitchell and Keith Smith; *Thirties Sutton* by Richard Essen; *Sutton United Football Club* by G.F. Buck and A.W. Letts; Church's *Directory of Sutton*; *The London Tramcar* by R.W. Kidner; *Now and Then* by Frank Burgess; *The Salvation Army, Sutton Corps Centenary 1886–1986*, and family albums and scrapbooks, especially those owned by my mother, Mrs Edith Tietjen, and my aunt, Mrs Kitty Burns.

Where necessary, copyright of pictures has been cleared if at all possible; apologies are tendered for any sources not fully dealt with or acknowledged.